Mind-Blowing

Quotes

Positively Disrupt Your Days

With Words

First Edition

Collected by

Philip Ryder Dunn

WORDS FOR DAILY MOTIVATION
AND INTENSE REFLECTION

QUOTES

DEEP

FOR

THOUGHTS

THINKERS

GIFTS OF WISDOM

Mind-Blowing Quotes

ISBN: 978-1986914819

Printed in the United States of America

Cover Design

Philip Ryder Dunn

Original Cover Artwork

Philip Ryder Dunn

Interior and Layout

Sperry Darden

Kendall Gaines

Philip Ryder Dunn

Web Development

Synapse Services Co.

synapsehub.com

Please send inquiries to pdunn@synapsehub.com

FORWARD

Gaining insight into another's mind is one of the more fascinating exercises of this life. We listen to the words, and often they strike a chord, a yearning or a spark in our own minds. We may have thought the same thing, or we become inspired to think differently because of the words and thoughts of another.

That's all we're doing here. This is a cherished collection of the web's most searched quotes. These gems are curated for your mind and the minds of those you share them with.

The sections are self-explanatory, and some quotes can go into multiple sections, of course. We just needed some organizing principle. Skip around and have a blast. If you want to look up quotes by author and page number, there's a handy index at the end of the book.

Please enjoy these quotes, use them in your own talks, works and travels, and allow them to expand your mind into areas untrodden. There's fun, humor, guidance, mysticism and jaw-dropping simplicity within these pages. Onwards!

— Philip Ryder Dunn, *quote collector*

INSPIRATION

"When you reach for the stars, you may not quite get one, but you won't come up with a handful of mud either."

– Leo Burnett

"A winner is someone who never lets losing stop them."

– unknown

"You cannot control how you feel, but you can always choose how you act."

– Mel Robbins

"A meaningful life can be extremely satisfying even in the midst of hardship, whereas a meaningless life is a terrible ordeal no matter how comfortable it is."

– Yuval Harari

"No one is useless in this world who lightens the burdens of another."

– Charles Dickens

"This is true in everyday life as it is in battle: we are given one life and the decision is ours whether to wait for circumstances to make up our mind, or whether to act and, in acting, to live."

– Omar Bradley

"In the depth of winter, I finally learned that within me there lay an invincible summer."

— *Albert Camus*

"Great things are not accomplished by those who yield to trends and fads and popular opinion."

— *Jack Kerouac*

"The things that matter most are not things."

— *Art Buchwald*

"Whatever you can do, or dream,
begin it. Boldness has genius, magic
and power in it. Begin it now."

*– Johann Wolfgang von
Goethe*

"Live as if you were to die
tomorrow. Learn as if you were to
live forever."

— Mahatma Gandhi

"The purpose of morality is to teach
you, not to suffer and die, but to
enjoy yourself and live."

– Ayn Rand

"Free yourself from the shackles of an oppressive reality. What's real to you is what you imagine and what you feel. If you manage your illusions wisely, you might get what you want, but you won't necessarily understand why it worked."

— Scott Adams

"Hem your blessings with thankfulness so they don't unravel."

— unknown

"I am not bound to win, but I am bound to be true. I am not bound to succeed, but I am bound to live by the light that I have. I must stand with anybody that stands right, and stand with him while he is right, and part with him when he goes wrong."

– Abraham Lincoln

"Today is a one time deal. Offer expires at midnight."

– Mike Dooley

"The smallest act of kindness is worth more than the grandest intention."

– Oscar Wilde

"I believe God is managing affairs and that He doesn't need any advice from me. With God in charge, I believe everything will work out for the best in the end. So what is there to worry about?"

– Henry Ford

"Bloom where you're planted."

– anonymous

"Optimism can make you look stupid, but cynicism always makes you look cynical."

– Calum Fisher

"Begin living like you've never lived before."

"Never underestimate the importance of having someone in your life who makes you want to be a better person."

– Dauvoire

"Don't Pursue Happiness – Create It."

– fortune cookie

"Those who attain to any excellence commonly spend life in some single pursuit, for excellence is not often gained from easier terms."

– Samuel Johnson

"For all my dreams, I am what I do."

– David Reynolds

"I greet the new sun with the confidence that this will be the best day of my life."

– Sperry Darden

"Have one breakthrough every day.
It's possible. Look for it."

– Kendall Gaines

"Joy is your birthright."

– Sarah Breathnach

"We are all in the gutter, but some
of us are looking at the stars."

– Oscar Wilde

"Now and then it's good to pause in our pursuit of happiness and just be happy."

– Guillaume Appollinaire

"Be bold in your caring, and be bold in your dreaming."

– George H.W. Bush

"Not everything that can be counted counts, and not everything that counts can be counted."

– Albert Einstein

"What is now proved was once only imagin'd"

– *William Blake*

"Having mastered the atom and the machinery of death that is modern warfare, the mere fact that we are alive now reveals a vast preference toward life and virtue."

– *Brendon Burchard*

"Don't try to make sense of it all, just go."

– *Rebelution*
(Comfort Zone)

"We can only be said to be alive in those moments when our hearts are conscious of our treasures."

– *Thornton Wilder*

"PINCH: Life isn't as serious as your mind makes it out to be."

– *Kendall Gaines*

"Everyone has access to really cool and really stupid information, media, education, stuff. . It's now more important than ever to train your attention and embrace only good."

– *Sperry Darden*

"And ah for a man to arise in me, That the man I am may cease to be!"

"Creative joy takes an artist's desperation. Place original work on the canvas of indifference and wait patiently."

– anonymous

"If there is a sin against life, it consists perhaps not so much in despairing of life as in hoping for another life and in eluding the implacable grandeur of this life."

– Albert Camus

"Perhaps the most severe requirement of the good life is to have the constancy of mind to maintain joy and gratitude even amid hardship, pain, and injustice."

– Brendon Burchard

"Live in each season as it passes;
breathe the air, drink the drink,
taste the fruit, and resign yourself
to the influences of each."

– Henry David Thoreau

"Let me first do some great thing
that shall be told among men
hereafter."

– Homer, The Iliad

"Twenty years from now you will be more disappointed by the things you didn't do than by the ones you did do... So throw off the bowlines. Sail away from the safe harbor. Catch the trade winds in your sails. Explore. Dream. Discover."

– Mark Twain

"Don't ask what the world needs. Ask what makes you come alive, and go do it. Because what the world needs is people who have come alive."

– Howard Thurman

"People of accomplishment rarely sit back and let things happen to them. They go out and happen to things."

– Leonardo Da Vinci

"Nature never said to me: Do not be poor; still less did she say: Be rich; her cry to me was always: Be independent."

– Nicolas Chamfort

"God is a verb."

– Buckminster Fuller

"There's no app for a bourbon buzz on a cool day in a warm, dark bar."

– Gone Girl

"Your generosity is more important than your perfection."

– Seth Godin

"Holding back is so close to stealing."

– Neil Young

"If you don't like something change it; if you can't change it, change the way you think about it."

— *Mary Engelbreit*

"In brief, sir, study what you most affect."

— *William Shakespeare*

"If you are going through hell, keep going."

— *Winston Churchill*

"If you want to feel good, be rational."

– *Ayn Rand*

"The secret to success is to subjugate your ego and serve others."

– *Stuart Wilde*

"A good plan today is better than a perfect plan tomorrow."

– *General George Patton*

"The universe is full of magical things patiently waiting for our wits to grow sharper."

— *Eden Phillpots*

"When everything seems to be going against you, remember that the airplane takes off against the wind, not with it."

— *Henry Ford*

"For every minute you are angry, you lose sixty seconds of happiness."

— *Ralph Waldo Emerson*

"Not my will but thine be done."

– New Testament

"Remember, a real decision is measured by the fact that you've taken new action. If there's no action, you haven't truly decided."

– Tony Robbins

"We go where our deepest desires take us."

– Deepak Chopra

"I not only use all the brains that I have, but all that I can borrow."

— *Woodrow Wilson*

"The less you know, the better you are at what you do know."

— *Kendall Gaines*

"The more that you read, the more things you will know. The more that you learn, the more places you'll go."

— *Dr. Seuss*

"Keep away from people who try to belittle your ambitions. Small people always do that, but the really great make you feel that you, too, can become great."

– *Mark Twain*

PROGRESS &
WORK

"If you're not willing to be a fool, then you can't be a master."

– *Jordan Peterson*

"The great eagle's nest is built of single sticks carefully placed."

– *P. King Dunn*

"Follow your blisters."

– *Joseph Campbell*

"The only cats worth anything are the cats that take chances."

– Thelonius Monk

"Create Like a God. Command Like a King. Work Like a Slave."

– Constantin Brancusi

"I rate enthusiasm even above professional skill."

— Edward Appleton

"You must have – in your heart – a commitment to customer service that goes beyond good sense and the desire for profits. It must be deep, and it must be strong, and it must endure."

– Mark Ford

"Play and pretend to work."

– Sperry Darden

"It's better to be a warrior in a garden than a gardener in a war."

– Martial arts story

"Perfection is finally attained not when there is no longer anything to add, but when there is no longer anything to take away."

– Antoine de Saint-Exupéry

"The reward of a thing well done is to have done it."

– Ralph Waldo Emerson

"If I had six hours to chop down a tree, I'd spend the first four sharpening the axe."

– Abe Lincoln

"Call on God, but row away from the rocks."

– *Hunter S. Thompson*

"The lack of plodding forward – not the lack of the ability to dream – is what makes a failure of the otherwise great human beings in this world."

– *unknown*

"The best work never was and never will be done for money."

– *John Ruskin*

"The feeling of happiness I had this morning – the kind that is good while you are working and gives you energy when you stop – comes only when: 1. You believe your work is meaningful. And. . . 2. You work at a relatively high level of competency."

– Mark Ford

"Doing is better than not doing, and if you do something badly you'll learn to do it better."

– Twyla Tharp

"To get what you never had,
you must do what you have
never done."

— *anonymous*

"What we call failure is not the
falling down but the staying down."

— *Mary Pickford*

"It is one of the most beautiful
compensations of this life that no
man can sincerely try to help
another without helping himself."

— *Ralph Waldo Emerson*

"An undefined problem has an indefinite number of solutions."

– Robert Humphrey

"No pressure, no diamonds."

– Thomas Carlyle

"If A is success in life, then A equals x plus y plus z. Work is x; y is play; and z is keeping your mouth shut."

– Albert Einstein

"Never hope more than you work."

– *Rita Mae Brown*

"In times of change, learners inherit the earth, while the learned find themselves beautifully equipped to deal with a world that no longer exists."

– *Eric Hoffer*

"Action is the foundational key to all success."

– *Pablo Picasso*

"Never compromise a dream.
Always compromise on how it will
come true."

> – *Mike Dooley*

"Out of the strain of the Doing. Into
the peace of the Done."

> - *Julia Louis Woodruff*

"One day, you will wake up and
there won't be any more time to do
the things you've always wanted.
Do it now."

> – *Paulo Coelho*

"Nothing is stronger than habit."

– Ovid

"The illiterate of the 21st century will not be those who cannot read and write, but those who cannot learn, unlearn, and relearn."

– Alvin Toffler

"Do whatever you have to do to keep things perfect in the moment. Just don't try."

– Sperry Darden

"To achieve great things, two things are needed: a plan, and not quite enough time."

– Leonard Bernstein

"Do or do not. There is no try."

– Yoda

"Little tiny dreams require little tiny thoughts and little tiny steps. Great big dreams require great big thoughts and little tiny steps."

– Mike Dooley

"Do what you do best, and outsource the rest."

– Peter Drucker

"I don't think there's anything to be afraid of. Failure brings great rewards — in the life of an artist."

– Quentin Tarantino

"There's no secret about success. Did you ever know a successful man who didn't tell you about it?"

– Kin Hubbard

"Early morning hath gold in its mouth."

"I didn't have all the expectations and the publicity. It probably made me work harder and learn more. It was a blessing in disguise."

– Dustin Penner – NHL Hockey Player (Anaheim Ducks) – on not being a stand-out talent

"If it's worth doing, it's worth doing
well. If it's worth doing, it's worth
doing badly."

> *– anonymous*

"The desire for safety stands
against every great and noble
enterprise."

> *– Tacitus*

"If the path before you is
clear, you're probably on
someone else's."

> *– C.G. Jung*

"Are you not ashamed that you give your attention to acquiring as much money as possible, and similarly with reputation and honor, and give no attention or thought to truth and understanding and the perfection of your soul?"

– Socrates

"Easy choices, hard life. Hard choices, easy life."

– Jerzy Gregorek

"I slept and dreamt that life was joy. I awoke and saw that life was service. I acted and beheld that service was joy."

– Tagore

"He that lives upon hope will die fasting."

– Benjamin Franklin

"By avoiding the process of creating and only consuming, you're denying the world your gifts."

– Jason Zook

"I don't know what your destiny will be, but one thing I know: the only ones among you who will be really happy are those who will have sought and found how to serve."

— *Albert Schweitzer*

"Every day you don't practice you're one day further from getting good."

— *anonymous*

"Struggle is a cherished consequence of higher actions. . the necessary effort of heroism and cultural advancement."

– *Brendon Burchard*

"He who has never failed is he who has never tried."

– *anonymous*

"The lure of the distant and the difficult is deceptive. The great opportunity is where you are."

— *John Burroughs*

"If you lack the will to start, you're already finished."

"The greatest discovery of my generation is that man can alter his life simply by altering his attitude of mind."

— *William James*

"Courting failure is the only way to advance."

– *Sperry Darden*

"Think of fear as a 2-year-old child who doesn't want to go grocery shopping with you. Because you must buy groceries, you'll just have to take the two year old with you. Fear is no different. In other words, acknowledge that fear exists but don't let it keep you from doing important tasks."

– Jack Canfield

"Think of the small as large."

– unknown

"Those that struggle with honor for mighty ends are not pitied but admired."

– Brendon Burchard

"Look at a day when you are supremely satisfied at the end. It's not a day when you lounge around doing nothing; it's when you've had everything to do, and you've done it."

– Margaret Thatcher

The End Result + Action = Hows + Manifestation

– Mike Dooley

"Find a subject you care about and
which you in your heart feel others
should care about. It is this genuine
caring, and not your games with
language, which will be the most
compelling and seductive element in
your style."

– Kurt Vonnegut

"Daily ingredients: Family, friends,
exercise, sun, work, music."

– Kendall Gaines

"Start by doing what's necessary; then
do what's possible; and suddenly you are
doing the impossible."

– St. Francis of Assisi

"Your ideas are your dogs. Love them, and give them your attention when they beg for it."

"Only our actions shall speak to who we are and what we really desire."

"Work like you don't need the money. Love like you've never been hurt. Dance like nobody's watching."

"..There is still an overwhelming social compulsion – an insanity of consensus, if you will – to get rich from life rather than live richly, to "do well" in the world instead of living well. And in spite of the fact that America is famous for its unhappy rich people, most of us remain convinced that just a little more money will set life right. In this way, the messianic metaphor of modern life becomes the lottery – that outside chance that the right odds will come together to liberate us from financial worries once and for all."

– Rolf Potts

"Nothing so liberalizes a man and expands the kindly instincts that nature put in him as travel and contact with many kinds of people."

– Mark Twain

"The function of abundance is not to possess things but to use them and gather experiences."

– Stuart Wilde

"When you come right down to it, the secret to having it all is loving it all."

– Dr. Joyce Brothers

"The best things in life must come by effort from within, not by gifts from the outside."

– Fred Corson

"It is those who concentrate on but one thing at a time who advance in this world. The great man or woman is the one who never steps outside his or her specialty or foolishly dissipates his or her individuality."

– Og Mandino

"If it was easy, everyone would be doing it, and you wouldn't have an opportunity."

– Bob Parsons

"I never knew an early-rising, hard-working, prudent man, careful of his earnings, and strictly honest who complained of bad luck."

– *Henry Ward Beecher*

"Success is moving from failure to failure with no loss of enthusiasm."

– *Winston Churchill*

"If you bake bread with indifference, you bake a bitter bread that feeds but half man's hunger."

– *Kahlil Gibran*

"Practice beats talent when talent doesn't practice."

– anonymous

"Tell me and I'll forget. Show me and I might not remember. Involve me, and I'll understand."

*– Native American
Proverb*

"Pleasure in the job puts perfection in the work."

– Aristotle

"Annuit coeptis"

> *– Providence has favored*
> *our undertakings.*

"Don't quit. Suffer now and live the rest of your life as a champion."

> *– Muhammad Ali*

"Those that know, do. Those that understand, teach."

> *– Aristotle*

"Do what you can, with what you have, where you are."

> *– Teddy Roosevelt*

"The one and only thing over which you have complete and total control is how you focus your own mind. Luckily, this determines everything else."

– Napoleon Hill

"Sometimes you have to be lucky, but I always say that to be lucky, you have to fight for it."

– Jonas Hiller (Anaheim Ducks goaltender)

"A pound of pluck is
worth a ton of luck."

*– James Garfield (but
then someone shot him)*

"I'm a great believer in luck, and I
find the harder I work the more I
have of it."

– Thomas Jefferson

TAO

"Life is a series of natural and spontaneous changes. Don't resist them – that only creates sorrow. Let reality be reality. Let things flow naturally forward in whatever way they like."

– Lao Tzu

"The Truth upholds the fragrant Earth and makes the living water wet. Truth makes fire burn and the air move, makes the sun shine and all life grow. A hidden truth supports everything. Find it and win."

– Ramayana

"Curving back upon My own
Nature, I create again and again."

– Bhagavad-Gita

"To be shaken out of the ruts of ordinary perception, to be shown for a few timeless hours the outer and the inner world, not as they appear to an animal obsessed with words and notions, but as they are apprehended directly and unconditionally, by Mind Large – this is an experience of inestimable value to everyone."

– Aldous Huxley

"Sell your presence and purchase bewilderment."

– Rumi

"I am a camera through which God creates and witnesses his world."

– Sperry Darden

"I have realized that the past and future are real illusions, that they exist in the present, which is what there is and all there is."

– Alan Watts

"No monkey mind."

– anonymous

"Outcome only improves when you ignore it and attend to the nitty gritty."

– Attentional Control in Tennis (John F. Murray Ph.D.)

"If you don't know where you're going, every road leads there."

– Tao saying

"People think they are doing various things, but actually Buddha is doing everything. Each one of us has many activities, but those activities are all Buddha's activities."

— *Shunryu Suzuki*

"It's so perfect here. Do whatever you have to do to keep it that way."

— *Kendall Gaines*

"Things fall apart; the centre cannot hold."

— *William Yeats*

"What lies behind us and what lies before us are small matters compared to what lies within us"

– *Ralph Waldo Emerson*

"Many things grow in the garden that were never sown there."

– *Thomas Fuller*

"Thought began to take over and obscured the simple yet profound joy of connectedness with being."

– *Eckhart Tolle*

"The man on top of the mountain did not fall there."

– unknown

"Men are disturbed not by things but by the principles and notions which they form concerning things."

– Epictetus

"It is so. It cannot be otherwise."

– Zen saying

"Nothing is more beautiful than something unusual."

– *Kendall Gaines*

"In all things of nature, there is something of the marvelous."

– *Aristotle*

"Men are disturbed not by the things that happen, but by their opinion of the things that happen."

– *Epictetus*

"What you encounter at your destination once you get there depends on the quality of this one step. Another way of putting it: What the future holds for you depends on your state of consciousness now."

— *Eckhart Tolle*

"Right now, the world is new."

— *Philip Penwid*

"They muddy the water, to make it seem deep."

— *Friedrich Nietzsche*

"The man who is truly good and wise will bear with dignity whatever fortune sends, and will always make the best of his circumstances."

– Aristotle

"When the basis for your actions is inner alignment with the present moment, your actions become empowered by the intelligence of Life itself."

– Eckhart Tolle

"When you've seen beyond
yourself, then you may find, peace
of mind is waiting there."

– George Harrison

"A man is whatever room he is in."

– Japanese saying

"The world is presenting wonders
by the minute. It's your job to
notice them. Witness them."

– Kendall Gaines

"The fullness of life is only accessible in the present moment."

– Eckhart Tolle

"There is no inside or outside for him. He reflects whatever appears, without judgement, whether it is a flower or a heap of garbage, a criminal or a saint. Whatever happens is alright. He treats his own anger or grief just as he would treat an angry or grieving child: with compassion."

– Tao Te Ching

"Reality is a unified whole, but thought cuts it up into fragments."

– Eckhart Tolle

"The reason we want to go on and on is because we live in an impoverished present."

– Alan Watts

"Expectation is the root of all heartache."

—William Shakespeare

"Life has no other discipline to impose, if we would but realize it, than to accept life unquestioningly. Everything... we deny, denigrate or despise, serves to defeat us in the end. What seems nasty, painful, evil, can become a source of beauty, joy and strength, if faced with an open mind. Every moment is golden for him who has the vision to realize it as such."

– Henry Miller

"One does not accumulate but eliminate. It is not daily increase but daily decrease. The height of cultivation always runs to simplicity."

– Bruce Lee

"Naturalness: You do not have to force yourself to drink water when you are thirsty; you are glad to drink water. Not Naturalness: When your mind is entangled in some other idea, someone else's idea, and you are not independent, not yourself, not natural."

– Shunryu Suzuki

"Assume the best, or don't assume anything."

– Philip Penwid

"The sky holds sun, moon, stars, clouds, rain, snow or pure azure. Because it doesn't care which of these appear, it has room for them all."

– Tao Te Ching

"Quality requires your Presence."

– Eckhart Tolle

"Zen does not confuse spirituality with thinking about God while one is peeling potatoes. Zen spirituality is just to peel the potatoes."

– Alan Watts

"What is this life if, full of care, we have no time to stand and stare."

– W.H. Davies

"The habit of being happy enables one to be freed, or largely freed, from the dominance of outward conditions."

– Robert Louis Stevenson

PSYCHOLOGY & ART

"That which you most need will be found where you least want to look."

– *Carl Jung*

"No sympathy for the devil; keep that in mind. Buy the ticket, take the ride...and if it occasionally gets a little heavier than what you had in mind, well...maybe chalk it up to forced consciousness expansion: Tune in, freak out, get beaten."

– *Hunter S. Thompson*

"For happiness, how little suffices
for happiness! . . . the least thing
precisely, the gentlest thing, the
lightest thing, a lizard's rustling, a
breath, a wisk, an eye glance – little
maketh up the best happiness. Be
still."

– Friedrich Nietzsche

"Do not seek the truth; only cease
to cherish opinions."

– Seng-ts'an

"We suffer more often in
imagination than in reality."

– Seneca

"The only good is knowledge and the only evil is ignorance."

– Socrates

"The more pleasures a man captures, the more masters he will have to serve."

– Seneca

"The more powerful and original a mind, the more it will incline towards the religion of solitude."

– Aldous Huxley

"Action follows desire."

– Napoleon Hill

"When the going gets weird, the weird turn pro."

– Hunter S. Thompson

"Until you make the unconscious conscious, it will direct your life, and you will call it fate."

– Carl Jung

"Trying to define yourself is like trying to bite your own teeth."

– Alan Watts

"The big question is whether you are going to be able to say a hearty yes to your adventure."

– Joseph Campbell

"You always have two choices: your commitment versus your fear."

– Sammy Davis Jr.

"Focus on the desired result."

– anonymous

"When you are unconscious, you are being thought by the collective mind."

– Eckhart Tolle

"Nor is it of much Importance to us to know the Manner in which Nature executes her laws; 'tis enough to know the Laws themselves."

– Ben Franklin

"Reality is causal."

– Ayn Rand

"Most people are about as happy as they make up their minds to be."

– Abraham Lincoln

"The only way to make sense out of change is to plunge into it, move with it, and join the dance."

– Alan Watts

"The hardest thing to explain is the glaringly evident which everybody has decided not to see."

– Ayn Rand

"Silent gratitude isn't much use to anyone."

– G.B. Stern

We judge the mystical experience not by its veracity, which is unknowable, but by its fruits: does it turn someone's life in a positive direction?

– William James
(paraphrased)

"The difference between genius
and stupidity is that genius has
its limits."

— *Albert Einstein*

"The fool who persists in his folly
becomes wise."

— *Robert Blake*

"The ego wants to want more than
it wants to have. And so the shallow
satisfaction of having is always
replaced by more wanting."

— *Eckhart Tolle*

"Dear God & Universe, You show me benign things. I make them good or bad and craft my experience."

"The best way to get approval is to not need it."

– Hugh MacLeod

"Great minds discuss ideas. Average minds discuss events. Small minds discuss people."

– Admiral Hyman Rickover (U.S. Navy)

"Circumstance has no value. It is how one relates to the situation that has value. All the meaning resides in the personal relationship to a phenomenon, what it means to you."

– Chris McCandless

"There is a level of cowardice lower than that of the conformist: the fashionable non-conformist."

– Ayn Rand

"As long as the ego runs your life, there are two ways of being unhappy. Not getting what you want. Getting what you want."

– Eckhart Tolle

"The happiness of those who want to be popular depends on others; the happiness of those who seek pleasure fluctuates with moods outside their control; but the happiness of the wise grows out of their own free acts."

– Marcus Aurelius

"We are never deceived; we deceive ourselves."

– Johann Wolfgang von Goethe

"Search others for their virtues."

– Benjamin Franklin

"Action without thought is mindlessness, and thought without action is hypocritical."

– Ayn Rand

"He that is good at making excuses is seldom good for anything else."

– Benjamin Franklin

"And people get all fouled up because they want the world to have meaning as if it were words…As if you had a meaning, as if you were a mere word, as if you were something that could be looked up in a dictionary. You are [the] meaning."

– Alan Watts

ART & PSYCHOLOGY

"Art and love are the same thing: It's the process of seeing yourself in things that are not you."

— *Chuck Klosterman*

"Everything you can imagine is real."

— *Pablo Picasso*

"Follow your inner moonlight; don't hide the madness."

— *Allen Ginsberg*

"In the age of Google and instant answers, the most compelling, fascinating thing is the human that can think on its feet (sans phone) and create story from recalled detail."

– Philip Penwid

"Art is 99 percent robbery."

– anonymous

"A weed is a treasure. With this attitude, whatever you do, life becomes an art."

– Shunryu Suzuki

"It's not what you look at that
matters, it's what you see."

– Henry David Thoreau

"Time and Space is where you
chase things you pretend you don't
have – love, friends, and
abundance – while worrying about
things you pretend you do have –
problems, challenges, and issues.
Until one day, you happen to notice
the prophetic powers of
pretending."

– Mike Dooley

"A short attention span makes all of your perceptions and relationships shallow and unsatisfying."

– Eckhart Tolle

"Our bravest and best lessons are not learned through success, but through misadventure. "

– Amos Bronson Alcott

"An idea is a feat of association."

– Robert Frost

"The inability to forget is far more devastating than the inability to remember."

– Mark Twain

"To acquire the habit of reading is to construct for yourself a refuge from almost all the miseries of life."

– W. Somerset Maugham

"Have nothing in your houses that you do not know to be useful or believe to be beautiful."

– William Morris

"Perhaps imagination is only intelligence having fun."

– *George Scialabra*

"Perfection is achieved not when there is nothing more to add, but when there is nothing left to take away."

– *Antoine de Saint-Exupery*

"The man who doesn't read good books has no advantage over the man who can't read them."

– *Mark Twain*

TIME

"Time is one of the most powerful influences on our thoughts, feelings, and actions, yet we are usually totally unaware of the effect of time in our lives."

– Philip Zimbardo

".. the monosyllable of the clock is Loss, loss, loss, unless you devote your heart to its opposition."

– Tennessee Williams

"I believe in coyotes and time as an abstract."

– R.E.M.

"Lack of time is the new poverty."

– anonymous

"For the ego to survive, it must make time – past and future – more important than the present moment."

– Eckhart Tolle

"Down to Gehenna, or up to the Throne, He travels the fastest who travels alone."

– Rudyard Kipling

"Giving up the illusion that you can predict the future is a very liberating moment. All you can do is give yourself the capacity to respond... the creation of that capacity is the purpose of strategy."

– Lord John Browne

"Drop the question of what tomorrow may bring, and count as profit every day that Fate allows you."

– Horace

YOUTH

"An inordinate passion for pleasure is the secret to remaining young."

– *Oscar Wilde*

"Fear is cured by the forced repetition of acts of courage."

– *Napoleon Hill*

"I don't know what this is about, but the best thing I can do for my sons and my daughters is to make it more livable."

– *Kendall Gaines*

"It takes a long time to grow young."

— *Pablo Picasso*

"This is the true joy of life, the being used for a purpose recognized by yourself as a mighty one… the being a force of Nature, instead of a feverish selfish little clod of ailments and grievances complaining that the world will not devote itself to making you happy."

— *George Bernard Shaw*

"Every failure brings with it the seed of an equivalent advantage."

– Napoleon Hill

"When your life changes, you must change. Or, when you change you must accept your self."

– Kendall Gaines

"If you think you're tops, you won't do much climbing."

— Arnold H. Glasgow

"The tragedy of old age is not that
one is old, but that one is young."

    – Oscar Wilde

"Adversity reveals character."

    – Curt Kovacs

"The underlying fear (and perhaps
loathing) of child rearing is that
we're teaching them to be adults."

    – Sperry Darden

"A person is not old until regrets take the place of dreams."

– John Barrymore

"The world has a habit of making room for the man whose words and actions show that he knows where he is going."

– Napoleon Hill

"Find out what you want. That's the hard part. Getting there is easy."

– Kendall Gaines

"Nothing that life has to offer is worth the price of worry."

– unknown

"If you can learn, you can change."

– unknown

"No man is whipped until he quits – in his own mind."

– Napoleon Hill

DEATH

"There is no life that is not ultimately frustrating."

— *Eckhart Tolle*

"Anyone ever lost in the wild knows that nature wants you dead."

— *David Mamet*

"Just beat my record for most consecutive days without dying."

— *Bill Murray*

"All men should strive to learn,
before they die, what they are
running from, and to, and why."

– James Thurber

"Life is not a journey to the grave
with the intention of arriving safely
in a nice and well-preserved body,
but rather to skid in broadside,
thoroughly used up, totally worn
out, and loudly proclaiming...
'Wow, what a ride!'"

– unknown

"So that his place shall never be with those cold and timid souls who knew neither victory nor defeat."

– Teddy Roosevelt

"The only completely consistent people are the dead."

– Aldous Huxley

POLITICS

"Disobedience is the true foundation of liberty. The obedient must be slaves."

– Henry David Thoreau

"It is useless to attempt to reason a man out of a thing he was never reasoned into."

– Jonathan Swift

"By giving us the opinions of the uneducated, journalism keeps us in touch with the ignorance of the community."

– Oscar Wilde

"The ego of the academy is blinding."

– Sperry Darden

"A liberal is someone who feels a great debt to his fellow man, which debt he proposes to pay off with your money."

– G. Gordon Liddy

"Politics is the art of achieving prestige and power without merit."

– P.J. O'Rourke

"Information is the oxygen of the modern age. It seeps through the walls topped by barbed wire, it wafts across the electrified borders."

– Ronald Reagan

"For those that will fight for it ...FREEDOM... has a flavor the protected shall never know."

– anonymous

"In my many years I have come to a conclusion that one useless man is a shame, two is a law firm and three or more is a congress."

– John Adams

"I contend that for a nation to try to tax itself into prosperity is like a man standing in a bucket and trying to lift himself up by the handle."

– Winston Churchill

"A government which robs Peter to pay Paul can always depend on the support of Paul."

– George Bernard Shaw

"Democracy must be something more than two wolves and a sheep voting on what to have for dinner."

– James Bovard

"Foreign aid might be defined as a
transfer of money from poor people
in rich countries to rich people in
poor countries."

> – *Douglas Casey*

"The smallest minority on earth is the
individual. Those who deny
individual rights cannot claim to be
defenders of minorities."

> – *Ayn Rand*

"Giving money and power to
government is like giving whiskey
and car keys to teenage boys."

> – *P.J. O'Rourke*

"Government is the great fiction, through which everybody endeavors to live at the expense of everybody else. "

– Frederic Bastiat

"Government's view of the economy could be summed up in a few short phrases: If it moves, tax it. If it keeps moving, regulate it. And if it stops moving, subsidize it."

– Ronald Reagan

"I don't make jokes. I just
watch the government and
report the facts."

– Will Rogers

"If you think health care is
expensive now, wait until you see
what it costs when it's free!"

– P.J. O'Rourke

"In general, the art of government
consists of taking as much money
as possible from one party of the
citizens to give to the other."

– Voltaire

"Just because you do not take an interest in politics doesn't mean politics won't take an interest in you!"

– Pericles (430 B.C.)

"No man's life, liberty, or property is safe while the legislature is in session."

– Mark Twain

"Talk is cheap…except when Congress does it."

– anonymous

"If you don't read the newspaper you are uninformed, if you do read the newspaper you are misinformed."

– Mark Twain

"The government is like a baby's alimentary canal, with a happy appetite at one end and no responsibility at the other."

– Ronald Reagan

"The only difference between a tax man and a taxidermist is that the taxidermist leaves the skin."

– Mark Twain

"What this country needs are more unemployed politicians."

– *Edward Langley*

"A government big enough to give you everything you want, is strong enough to take everything you have."

– *Thomas Jefferson*

"Suppose you were an idiot. And suppose you were a member of Congress. But then I repeat myself."

– *Mark Twain*

"Individual rights are the means of subordinating society to moral law."

– Ayn Rand

"There is no distinctly native American criminal class...save Congress."

– Mark Twain

"A democracy cannot exist as a permanent form of government. It can only exist until the voters discover that they can vote themselves money from the public treasury."

– Alexander Tyler

ECONOMY

"Here in the rich world, the only widespread form of slavery is the economic type."

– Mr. Money Moustache

Mistake: "Gauging one's worth by what one possesses rather than who one is."

– Michael Paterniti

"People will give you their time if you give them something valuable in exchange for it."

– anonymous

"The inherent vice of capitalism is the unequal sharing of the blessings. The inherent blessing of socialism is the equal sharing of misery."

– *Winston Churchill*

"All you have shall some day be given. Therefore give now, that the season of giving may be yours and not your inheritors."

– *Kahlil Gibran*

"So you think that money is the root of all evil. Have you ever asked what is the root of all money?"

– Ayn Rand

"A part of all I earn is mine to keep."

– anonymous

"If you have a talent, spend it lavishly like a millionaire intent on going broke."

– Brendan Francis

"By placing a lot of emotion into having, you heighten not having (and make yourself poorer)."

— *Stuart Wilde*

"Be a producer, not a consumer."

— *Sperry Darden*

"The most valuable thing that money can buy you is the freedom to spend your time as you see fit."

— *Michael Masterson*

"When it's a question of money,
everybody is of the same religion."

– Voltaire

"Every government interference
in the economy consists of giving
an unearned benefit, extorted by
force, to some men at the
expense of others."

– Ayn Rand

"It's not so hard to get rich as it
is to know when you have
gotten rich."

– Josh Billings

"Lack of money is the root
of all evil."

– George Bernard Shaw

"Money is only a tool. It will take
you wherever you wish, but it will
not replace you as the driver."

– Ayn Rand

"What we obtain too cheap, we
esteem too lightly."

– Thomas Paine

"Normal is getting dressed in clothes that you buy for work and driving through traffic in a car that you are still paying for – in order to get to the job you need to pay for the clothes and the car, and the house you leave vacant all day so you can afford to live in it."

– Ellen Goodman

"Run for your life from any man who tells you that money is evil. That sentence is the leper's bell of an approaching looter."

– Ayn Rand

"If money is your hope for independence you will never have it. The only real security that a man will have in this world is a reserve of knowledge, experience, and ability."

– *Henry Ford*

"True wealth is not what you have, it's what you're left with when all you have is gone."

– *James Ray*

ADVERTISING & MARKETING

"People don't ask for facts in making up their minds. They would rather have one good, soul-satisfying emotion . . ."

– Robert Keith Leavitt

"Ours has become a world where a tragic number of people have become more fascinated by materialism and the lives of distant narcissists than by their own life experience."

– Brendon Burchard

"Imagination is its own form of courage."

– House of Cards

"Advertising arguments should only be settled by testing, not arguments around a conference table."

– Claude Hopkins

"Arouse in the other person an eager want."

– Dale Carnegie

"The world is ruled and the destiny
of civilization is established by the
human emotions."

— *Napoleon Hill*

"People who are obsessed with
appearance are the ones most likely
to be fooled by it."

— *anonymous*

"If it doesn't sell, it isn't creative."

— *David Ogilvy*

"Core selling ideas: Who are you?
What are you doing? Who are you
helping? How are you different?"

"Great marketing only makes a bad
product fail faster."

– David Ogilvy

"Make promises. List benefits.
Create attractive images."

– Marketing mantra

"Netflix did it right and focused on all the things that have replaced the dumb, raw numbers of the Nielsen world — they embraced targeted marketing and 'brand' as a virtue higher than ratings."

– Kevin Spacey

"Advertising will only accelerate what was going to happen anyway."

– anonymous

"In good times, people want to advertise; in bad times, they have to."

– Bruce Barton

"Make buying from you a pleasure. Make seeing you a pleasure. Make hearing your voice on the phone a pleasure. Make everything about being with you a pleasure. Make a difference in your world. In the moment."

– unknown

HUMOR

"The children are our future,' which is true, but they said that when I was a child. Then I grew up. I was like 'here I am!' They were like, 'Now it's the other kids.' ...I know a Ponzi scheme when I see one..."

– *Norm MacDonald*

"Everything in the world is about sex except sex. Sex is about power."

– *Oscar Wilde*

"Fear is freedom! Subjugation is liberation! Contradiction is truth! Those are the facts of this world! And you will all surrender to them, you pigs in human clothing!"

— *Satsuki*

"He who throws mud only loses ground."

— *Fat Albert*

"The problem with the world is that the intelligent people are full of doubts, while the stupid ones are full of confidence."

— *Charles Bukowski*

"Spilling a full beer you paid for is
the adult equivalent of letting go of
a balloon."

"Humor is just another defense
against the universe."

– *Mel Brooks*

"Every great cause begins as a
movement, becomes a business,
and eventually degenerates into a
racket."

– *Eric Hoffer*

"When I die, I hope to go to Heaven, whatever the Hell that is."

— *Ayn Rand*

"The human race has only one really effective weapon, and that is laughter. The moment it arises, all our hardnesses yield, all our irritations and resentments slip away and a sunny spirit takes their place."

— *Mark Twain*

"Don't give advice. Dumb people don't take it, and smart people don't need it."

"If people never did silly things, nothing intelligent would ever get done."

– Ludwig Wittgenstein

"There are three ways to get something done: Do it yourself, employ someone, or forbid your children to do it."

– Montana Crane

"Everyone wants to be a part of a miracle. I turned a corner. She's a part of it. People helping people. It's powerful stuff."

— *Wedding Crashers*

"The reward for conformity is that everyone likes you but yourself."

— *Rita Mae Brown*

"To mistrust science and deny the validity of the scientific method is to resign your job as a human. You'd better go look for work as a plant or wild animal."

— *P. J. O'Rourke*

"My first editor once told me that whenever you think you see malice or conspiracy, you're probably just seeing incompetence."

– *Mike Elgan*

"Never attribute to malice that which is adequately explained by stupidity."

– *Robert J. Hanlon*

"I'm not normally a religious man, but if you're up there, save me, Superman!"

– *Homer Simpson*

"Intelligence is like four-wheel drive .. it just gets you stuck in more remote places."

— *Garrison Keillor*

"In the end, everything will work out. And if it doesn't then it's not the end yet."

— *anonymous*

"The ultimate result of shielding men from the effects of folly is to fill the world with fools."

— *Herbert Spencer*

"More than any other time in history, mankind faces a crossroads. One path leads to despair and utter hopelessness. The other, to total extinction.
Let us pray we have the wisdom to choose correctly."

– Woody Allen

"If you really want something in life you have to work for it. Now quiet, they're about to announce the lottery numbers."

– Homer Simpson

"Bacon is the Chuck Norris of food.
There's no reviewing it. It's bacon.
It reviews you. Now go."

– anonymous

"A bore is a person who opens his
mouth and puts his feats in it."

– Henry Ford

"Trying is the first step
towards failure."

– Homer Simpson

"When I write, I feel like an armless, legless man with a crayon in his mouth."

– *Kurt Vonnegut*

"I think people place too much emphasis on their careers. I wish we could all live in the mountains."

– *Bill Murray,*
Groundhog Day

"Pay no attention to the critics. Don't even ignore them."

– *Samuel Goldwyn*

"To alcohol! The cause of and
solution to all of life's problems!"

– Homer Simpson

"The truth will set you free, but
first it will piss you off."

– Werner Erhard

"OK brain. You don't like me, and I
don't like you, but let's get through
this thing and then I can continue
killing you with beer."

– Homer Simpson

"The best ideas come as jokes.
Make your thinking as funny as
possible."

– *David Ogilvy*

AUTHOR INDEX

A

B

Barrymore

     John, 100

Barton

     Bruce, 129

Bastiat

     Frederic, 110

Beecher

     Henry Ward, **53**

Bernstein

     Leonard, 37

Bhagavad-Gita, **59**

Billings

     Josh, 121

Blake

     Robert, 82

     William, 12

Bovard

     James, 108

Bradley

     Omar, 2

Brancusi

     Constantin, 27

Breathnach

     Sarah, 10

Brooks

     Mel, 133

Brothers

        Dr. Joyce, 51

Brown

        Rita Mae, 34, 136

Browne

        Lord John, **95**

Buchwald

        Art, 3

Burchard

        Brendon, 12, 15, 44, 47, 49, 125

Burnett

        Leo, 1

Burroughs

        John, **44**

Bush

        George H.W., 11

C

Campbell

        Joseph, **26**, **78**

Camus

        Albert, 3, 15

Canfield

        Jack, **46**

Carlyle

        Thomas, 33

Carnegie

        Dale, 126

D

L

M

McCandless

 Chris, **84**

Miller

 Henry, 70

Monk

 Thelonius, 27

Morris

 William, **91**

Moustache

 Mr. Money, 117

Murray

 Bill, 61, 102, 141

N

Native American Proverb, **54**

New Testament, 23

Nietzsche

 Friedrich, 66, 75

O

O'Rourke

 P.J., 106, 109, 111, 136

Ogilvy

 David, 127, *128*, 143

Ovid, 36

R

S

Tyler

>Alexander, 116

U

unknown, 1, 5, 30, 45, 46, 64, 101, 103, 130, 133

V

Voltaire, 111, 121

Vonnegut

>Kurt, 48, 141

W

Watts

>Alan, **60**, **70**, **73**, **78**, **80**, 86

Wedding Crashers, 136

Wilde

>Oscar, 6, 10, 96, 99, 105, 120, 131

>Stuart, 21, **51**

Wilder

>Thornton, 13

Williams

>Tennessee, **93**

Wilson

>Woodrow, 24

Wittgenstein

>Ludwig, 135

Woodruff

Julia Louis, 35

Y

Yeats

William, 62

Yoda, **37**

Young

Neil, 19

Z

Zen saying, **64**

Zimbardo

Philip, **93**

Zook

Jason, **42**

www.ingramcontent.com/pod-product-compliance
Lightning Source LLC
Chambersburg PA
CBHW061636250726
48659CB00004B/1253